# Never Enough Time

A Feel Good Through the Grief Book,
Losing Not Only a Member of Your
Family, but a Best Friend

**Lane Michaels**

# Table of Contents

# Introduction

I'll never forget the day my family brought Si home, a rambunctious, fat little black Lab puppy. His big brown eyes peered up at me as his tail wagged excitedly. At that moment, I knew our lives would forever be changed.

Over the next ten years, Si and I formed an unbreakable bond built on unconditional love and trust. He was by my side as I navigated childhood, adolescence, and young adulthood. On my toughest days, I found comfort curled up with him as he showered me with sloppy kisses. On my happiest days, we played endless hours of fetch in the backyard as the sunshine beamed down.

Si wasn't just a pet to me—he was a confidant, a protector, and, most importantly, my best friend. The depth of our connection amazed me every day. He understood me better than any human ever could.

So when Si's health started deteriorating last year, my heart shattered into a million pieces. Over those excruciating last few months, I found myself dreading when his suffering would end while simultaneously praying his pain would cease. I wasn't ready to lose my best friend, but I also couldn't bear to see him suffer.

On a quiet September morning, we said our final goodbyes as the veterinarian gently helped Si pass on. I was devastated in a way I had never experienced before. My world suddenly felt darker and colder without his familiar, comforting presence.

# Chapter 1:

# It's Okay to Grieve

In the weeks after Si's death, I was lost in waves of grief I struggled to process. It felt like I was all alone without my constant companion, who was always with me in my times of sorrow. Who else could comfort me the way he did? Countless questions ran through my head: Had we made the right decision? Was there something more we could have done to save my loyal friend? Although the vet continually reassured us we had done everything possible to save my beloved pal and that putting him down would finally end his suffering, the questions still arose.

On that dreadful day, as we said our goodbyes, it was one of the hardest days of my life. I remember as I held him in my arms, feeling his faint heartbeat and labored breathing, my own heart shattered into a million pieces. Laying Si's body to rest was like losing a part of myself, the very best part. Walking out of the clinic without him by my side, empty collar in hand, I was nowhere near close to facing the reality of what had just occurred.

I know all of my family was grieving; each one lost the family member that Si was to them as well. The ride home was quiet. The only sound to be heard was that of sniffles and faint sobs.

In the weeks that followed, I struggled to make sense of a world without my faithful companion. Navigating the chaos of grief became an exhausting rollercoaster, amplified by well-meaning loved ones insisting it would get easier and to just get another dog. Their dismissiveness cut deep, invalidating the profound pain of losing someone so special.

My immediate family was reeling in their own ways. Dad was being strong while assuring us we would get another "great" dog in time. Mom was trying to console all with hugs while hiding away her own tears, dying inside at the loss of what was also her "pet" child.

I knew Si wouldn't want me to be sad. He'd want me to remember our bond and feel complete happiness, knowing he was no longer in pain. My mind flashed with images of him looking up at me with those big brown eyes—oh, how I missed them already. The struggle of trying to learn to be happy without him was a daunting task I knew we all had to face.

Although this has been a long road, and even today, a tear will escape my eye as I think of him. I want you to know that not only is it okay to grieve, but it's also healthy. It puts into perspective how much you really loved them. Some people won't understand the profound pain of losing a pet. "He was just a dog," they'll say, failing to grasp what he meant to me. I pity them for not knowing the true loyalty and love a pet can bring when you share such a connection.

Through my grieving, in time, I found solace in the memories Si and I created over the years. As I thumbed through photo albums celebrating his silly antics, our quiet cuddle sessions, and adventures, a glimmer of peace washed over me. With each fond memory came a wave of nostalgia, and soon, the cold hollow in my chest softened. He was many a topic of family dinner conversations, with lots of laughs and slight bittersweet pangs of sorrow. Each of us had vivid memories to add to each other's stories. Pictures adorn our home, and the laughter he still incites makes every day a comforting reminder of his beautiful soul.

The love between humans and their animal companions is truly extraordinary. Our pets captivate our hearts and infiltrate our souls in a profound way few human relationships ever achieve.

Pets provide endless affection and wholeheartedly accept us as we are. They ease our worries through their soothing presence and make even the worst days brighter. Our animal friends forge an unbreakable bond most people cherish for a lifetime.

## The Evolution of the Family Dynamic

Initially, pets join households as wide-eyed additions shuffling awkwardly about, discovering their niche. Early days overflow with challenges like behavioral corrections, veterinary needs, and lifestyle adjustments to better suit our furry friends. Some temporarily reconsider their readiness to assume responsibility for dependent beings.

Yet devotion wins out. As months pass, amusing quirks endear these newcomers into trusted confidants. Their needs shape familiar routines as they transition slowly from outsiders to insiders within our inner circles. Soon, they know our needs better than we articulate them ourselves.

Gradually, euphoria hits as one realizes that this adoption expanded one's family in the best possible way. Thanks to their spirited antics, laughter permeates days constantly. Scampering paws rush eagerly to offer affection following any absence as if disappearing even briefly constitutes a minor tragedy in their world. Their steadfast delight in greeting your daily homecoming mirrors the joy they awakened in your own heart, too.

It becomes hard to imagine a car ride or bathroom break without them. Over the years, beds inched closer until you woke nose-towet-nose. Lazy weekends no longer motivate adventures further than the couch or a sunny patch of grass in the backyard, that is, unless family travels include your furry friend. Their familiar presence assumes irreplaceable status, conveying wordless empathy on hard days that no human could fully replicate.

## Challenges and Learning Curves

Welcoming wide-eyed newcomers into one's tribe sounds ideal. But reality tests commitment through harsh challenges and sacrifices as former orderly households adapt to accommodate a new needy pet. Sleepless nights alternate with daily irritation over behaviors requiring correction and discipline, like gnawed table legs, torn shoes, or countless accidents. Preserving treasured belongings means relocation until proper training establishes house rules. Fights ensue over whose turn it is for walks or baths, and of course, whose pet it actually is when the messes occur.

Financial investments soar while adjusting budgets for vet visits, food, and boarding costs. Finding pet-friendly housing shrinks relocation options. Fantasies of restful vacations sans responsibilities when welcoming your new adoptee. Will they be able to join, or will we be able to find the most trustworthy pet sitter?

Some question whether trading tranquility for such chaos proves wise in the long term. Yet, for all fur-related frustrations, unconditional affection changes everything. Love's steadfast power inspires protecting these vulnerable beings who view you as their whole world. With consistent nurturing, trying times transition into trusts built to last.

# Becoming a Family

Though we had only just met, an instant bond blossomed between us that day we brought him home. Little did I know the profound role this goofy bundle of fur would come to play in our family, worming his way into our hearts to become like a child to nurture and cherish for life.

As Si grew from an awkward puppy to a loyal companion always by my side, the changes to our family dynamic proved subtly transformative. His needs dictated daily routines like mealtimes and walks, ever strengthening our home's foundation. His affectionate nature as a resident "therapy dog" lifted spirits on the toughest days. Laughter permeated those days, playing silly games that challenged our anxiety. Over time, Si simply became an integral member no different than human relatives.

Navigating those early challenges from chewed-up shoes to potty training tested commitment. But embracing unconditional love made all compromises worthwhile. Eventually, Si felt less like a pet and more like a kindred spirit, illuminating each moment shared with joy.

Losing this cherished family member who offered such security and comfort over a decade unleashes intense, unfillable yearning. Yet Si showed relationships without words are equally profound. I rediscovered peace by remembering the extraordinary familial bond we built nurturing this sweet pup from childhood to adulthood, knowing I was blessed to love someone so deeply. Our connection forever changed how I define family going forward.

Please take the time to think back on those trying, turbulent, yet wonderful days.

# Chapter 2:

# Your Grief Is Valid

*Grief is the price we pay for love.* –Queen Elizabeth II

An increasing body of research demonstrates how animal companionship offers tremendous psychological and physical benefits. Pet owners often exhibit lower stress levels, heart rates, and blood pressure than non-pet owners. Pets alleviate anxiety and feelings of loneliness while boosting moods. Stroking a purring cat or cuddling a content puppy releases oxytocin, the "feel good" hormone promoting affectionate bonds. Animals can even strengthen our immune systems and lower the risk of certain illnesses.

Beyond the positive impacts, animals fill an emotional need to nurture and bond closely with another living being. Their presence brings out our best qualities, like playfulness, patience, and love. Life with a devoted pet overflows with laughs, cozy snuggles, and heartwarming moments—a perfect recipe for a lasting friendship.

With such profound connections formed, losing a beloved animal companion causes deep grief and painful adjustments. Yet the diverse benefits of pet relationships demonstrate why we repeatedly welcome animals into our hearts despite the inevitable sorrow when we must say goodbye.

Losing your dearest furry friend leaves you reeling in a state of overwhelming grief and heartache. Waves of sadness, anger, guilt, loneliness, and longing crash over you as you try to grasp a new reality without their comforting presence.

Navigating such immense sorrow is a challenging, lonely road. Know that your grief represents the depth of your love and bond with your precious pet. By mourning their loss, you honor their memory and the irreplaceable role they played in your life.

I wrote this book to help you through the grieving journey of losing a beloved animal companion. Consider this a supportive guide through the darkest valleys of grief—until joyful memories replace sadness and you rediscover peace.

Within these pages, I validate the profound pain you're experiencing. While reminiscing about your relationship's special moments, think about how cherished memories can lift your spirits. Reflecting on your pet's unique paw print on your heart brings catharsis amidst the pain.

I won't rush your healing or undermine the significance of your loss. Instead, take things step-by-step, riding out waves of grief as they crash and bask in soothing memories when the waters calm. Be patient with yourself, surround yourself with compassion, and know you don't have to walk this excruciating path alone.

## Acknowledge the Pain

Losing your faithful companion leaves you with a gaping hole in your heart that no one and no thing can instantly fill. Your pet occupied a special role—as a family member, confidant, protector, therapist, adventure buddy, cuddle partner, and conduit of unconditional love. Their familiar presence wove through every facet of your daily life, large and small.

With their absence, your days now feel off-kilter and hollow. The pain haunts your waking moments and keeps you up at night. Every reminder conjures fresh waves of heartache—stray balls of fur around the house, glancing at their empty beds, stumbling upon a beloved toy they'll never again play with.

I won't tell you to snap out of your grief or stop crying. Nor will I utter hollow sentiments like, "It was just a pet." Pets aren't disposable objects—they're living beings occupying central roles in our hearts and homes. Your anguish directly reflects how deeply your pet's life and love were intertwined with yours.

Grieving is the necessary, natural response to losing someone so precious. By giving yourself permission to fully experience the mourning process, you honor their memory. Denying or bottling up emotions often worsens and prolongs pain. I promise better days lie ahead, my friend. For now, embrace the darkness, knowing light still flickers within. You'll get through this, one moment at a time.

## Understanding Pet Grief as a Valid Emotion

It's just a dog/cat/pet.

How often do grieving pet owners hear those diminishing words said with pity, judgment, or dismissal? Far too often, society fails to recognize the legitimacy of pet grief and how viscerally losing animal companions devastates those left behind.

Some people treat animal loss as qualitatively lesser than human loss. Hence, the insensitive platitudes that minimize painful emotions. Others can't relate as they've never experienced that special reciprocal bond with pets enriching their daily lives.

Make no mistake: Grief over losing a cherished pet is deep, real, and messy. It's no different than grieving a human loved one. Pets permeate our hearts, homes, and daily routines over the years or decades through their steadfast companionship. We pour boundless time, affection, care, resources, laughter, and tears into nurturing these relationships. That level of emotional intimacy spanning years understandably inflicts profound grief when permanently severed.

Consider Traci, who was inconsolable when she lost Molly, her giant black pound dog. Molly saw Traci through hard days of parenting and even harder days at work. That goofy, affectionate ball of fur comforted Traci daily, making her feel safe, loved, and worthy.

Losing Molly left Traci feeling utterly alone in facing life's struggles without her faithful, unconditional ally.

Or Tom, whose elderly calico cat Hank was his only source of warmth and affection amidst struggling finances, social isolation, and depression after a messy divorce. With Hank gone, Tom lost his sweet, purring therapy cat and sole daily companion.

The grief Traci, Tom, and so many others experience after losing beloved pets is valid and real. My goal for this book is to help you embrace these painful emotions, knowing you aren't alone.

Each memory, no matter how small, immortalizes your pet's legacy. Revisiting them through the lens of love eternally etches their paw print into your heart. Bit by bit, laughter edges out the loneliness until those memories predominantly glow with joy instead of ache.

Reflecting on your favorite memories together—those that shaped your bond or captured your pet's essence—brings bittersweet pangs. Yet recalling their quirky personality, heartwarming gestures, and silly antics evokes nostalgic smiles, too. Soon, chuckles will emerge as you picture earlier moments of joy you shared.

Remember the time your pup mischievously grabbed your leftovers off the counter when you stepped away? Or how your kitten raced and slid across the hardwood floors while chasing the laser light, or when your elderly pet snuggled up extra close on days sensing your anxiety? These are memories that need to be cherished.

# Chapter 3:

# Take the Time

Never feel ashamed for needing time and space to process this immense loss in your own way. Emotions manifest differently for everyone after a major life change. Create an environment nurturing your unique grieving process without self-judgment.

Protect time for mourning rituals that bring you comfort: Look through old photos or videos, write letters to your pet, and create a memorial space displaying their collar or ashes. Seek support by connecting with others experiencing similar heartache. Not surprisingly, the world is full of people who truly mourn the loss of their own pets like you.

Most importantly, give yourself unlimited grace, empathy, and compassion. Ignore any timeline dictating "appropriate" grieving periods. Healing happens gradually, fueled by self-care and small steps forward.

The journey ahead contains unpredictable twists and turns as you learn to live without your faithful companion. Mourning their loss spans a rollercoaster of emotions ranging from denial, anger, loneliness, and guilt to occasional laughter while reminiscing joyful times together. Through various coping strategies and support systems, including this guide, you'll discover brighter days.

While I can't predict exactly how your personal grief journey will unfold, I can promise you that you are not alone.

Rather than rushing your healing, take things step-by-step at your pace. Some days, give yourself permission to collapse in a puddle of tears. On other days, go on a long nature walk, one they would have loved.

Just know there is no "right" way to grieve. Embrace what feels authentic in your season of this process. With compassion as your guide, it may help lift the darkness.

Your role in this journey is knowing that healing starts from within, through courageously facing emotions and putting in self-work.

Throughout this book, ask yourself thought-provoking questions to prompt meaningful reflection.

Pick strategies that resonate most powerfully with you and practice them with regularity. Healing resembles a winding path rather than an overnight solution. But with daily upkeep, you'll grow stronger.

Most importantly, believe you deserve happiness again. It won't look the same, but your pet would want you thriving after the initial mourning period passes.

# Chapter 4:

# Exploring the Depths of Grief

Grief is a natural, complex human response to any loss, severing emotional attachments. Though often associated with death, grief transcends beyond bereavement to incorporate endings of all kinds—divorces, breakups, job losses, relocations, or transitions.

Psychologists describe acute grief as an intense, concentrated burst of mourning endured in the initial aftermath of a loss. As the reality of absence sets in, acute grief unleashes a visceral spectrum of thoughts and emotions. Acute grief gradually transitions into integrated grief characterized by adapting to loss through cherishing positive memories and discovering hope for the future.

However, for some like myself, struggling to reconcile a loved one's absence from my daily life, acute grief persists long-term as prolonged or complicated grief. Hallmarks of prolonged grief include yearning or longing, disbelief, avoidance, bitterness, emotional numbness or detachment, lost sense of purpose, or difficulty envisioning a fulfilling life without the deceased. Prolonged grief impedes healing by entrapping people in relentless, painful rumination. Seeking professional counseling aids the journey toward acceptance and peace. As a society, we are ashamed of the thought of wanting or needing "counseling" in order to process our emotions. However, depression is a very real thing and is becoming more prevalent in the world as it is today.

Regardless of duration, grieving is neither linear nor predictable but rather a chaotic cycle between many responses. By better comprehending grief's variability and respecting your unique mourning process, you empower mindful navigation of the tumultuous waters ahead.

# The Emotional Spectrum

Few human experiences elicit such a vast spectrum of emotions as grief. Mourning the loss of beloved pets like Si elicits especially intense, devastating reactions, given their intimate daily presence and unconditional love.

Common emotions accompanying acute grief include:

- shock and disbelief

- numbness

- sadness

- yearning

- loneliness

- fatigue

- irritability

- bitterness

- helplessness

As the reality of loss sinks in, intense pangs of grief may feel literally breathtaking, gripping your chest like a vice. Sobs can erupt unexpectedly, triggered by seemingly harmless reminders—glancing at your pet's worn leash hanging by the door, seeing the scratched-up couch, or catching a whiff of their favorite treats.

Overwhelming heartache may give way to outbursts of rage at the injustice and meaninglessness of death. "How could this happen?" we scream internally "Life is so unfair!" Bouts of sobbing and stoic silence may alternate for stretches; appetites may vanish, and sleep escapes.

In rare interludes, flickers of light penetrate the darkness—a chuckle upon remembering your pet's silly gestures or your heart warming at old photos capturing your special bond. Within the hurricane of grief lie gentle moments of respite when cherished memories temper the anguish.

By naming these emotions rather than judging them, we strip away shame and validate grief's legitimacy. Our pets occupy irreplaceable roles in our lives; therefore, mourning their absence through varied, unpredictable reactions demonstrates the depth of love and meaning within those relationships.

# The Stages of Grief

Pioneering psychiatrist Elisabeth Kübler-Ross first coined the five stages of grief in 1969 based on learnings with terminally ill patients:

## *Denial*

Denial acts as an initial buffer, emotionally insulating people from the harsh bite of loss. You may unconsciously reject loss by pretending nothing changed or irrationally believing you'll reunite with the deceased. Denial helps stagger the blow's intensity but impedes the processing of other grief stages necessary for healing.

## *Anger*

Intense heartache gives way to misplaced fury aimed inwardly through guilt or outward toward authority figures, fate, or the deceased. Recognizing anger masks vulnerability from the injustice of death. Channeling anger into memorializing your pet through scrapbooks or donations honors their memory.

## Bargaining

Grasping for control amidst chaos, some people irrationally bargain with deities to reverse fate in exchange for moral righteousness. Bargaining exemplifies magical thinking that cannot alter reality. Find empowerment in actions uplifting your pet's enduring legacy over elements beyond control.

## Depression

As denial, anger, and bargaining smoke screens lift, grief's excruciating weight often manifests as devastating depression. Symptoms like perpetual sadness, poor concentration, and altered sleep and appetite patterns require self-care and social support to prevent lasting impairment. Light lurks ahead if you forge bravely onward.

## Acceptance

With compassion and courage, glassy waves of grieving gradually calm, establishing equilibrium between sorrow and solace. Cherishing your relationship's many blessings balances yearning for impossibilities. You honor your pet's enduring gift by rediscovering laughter and purpose.

Grief rarely unfolds linearly through these stages but rather unpredictably oscillates between them for months or years. Recognizing when perceptions align with a certain stage's hallmarks demystifies their chaos, validating your reactions as normal. Be gentle with yourself when the darkness descends, knowing you don't walk alone.

# Chapter 5:

# The Physical Manifestations

# of Grief

The mind–body connection means grief's emotional upheaval unleashes a cascade of physical consequences. Especially when grieving deeply for months on end, chronic stress taxes multiple body systems. Physical symptoms accompanying prolonged grief involve:

- headaches

- muscle weakness

- chest tightness

- digestive issues like nausea or changes in appetite

- increased infections from a weakened immune system

- disrupted sleep cycles, leaving you fatigued

- lethargy and low motivation

- actually feeling heartache—increased cardiovascular risks

Take part in gentle self-care like resting, hydrating, exercising moderately, embracing emotions, and asking for help navigating the stormy seas ahead when waves of grief capsize you.

No universally "right" method exists for processing loss, but denying grief guarantees prolonged agony. Face life's turbulent tides of sorrow and joy alike to rediscover stillness. However uniquely grief touches you, construct meaning from the wreckage until positivity permeates the pain. Si's enduring gift of love is teaching me that the brokenhearted can still breathe, dream, and heal in time's merciful passage. Cherish this wisdom as your faithful companion, illuminating the way home from darkness.

# The Impact of Pet Loss on Mental Health

Losing a beloved pet inflicts intense emotional wounds that profoundly impact mental health. Grief manifests through complex psychological reactions like yearning, sorrow, guilt, anger, and loneliness. Physical symptoms often accompany mental anguish, including fatigue, insomnia, changed appetite, digestive issues, or headaches.

Caregivers tending to dying pets often witness immense suffering, which worsens their traumatic loss reactions. Elderly owners, singles lacking social support, and those heavily depending on pets for security frequently spiral into despair. The key is catching their grief early and offering compassionate care to nurture healing.

Through psychotherapy techniques like narrative sharing, memory work, and cognitive restructuring to challenge problematic thought patterns, most rediscover hope. Support groups validate struggles and inspire resilience-building coping skills. Many emerge renewed with cherished memories gleaming brighter than pain.

# Reflection Questions:

1. What emotions have dominated your grief experience so far? How have you found healthy outlets to process them? Consider journaling or support groups.

2. In what ways has your cultural or spiritual upbringing shaped your perspectives on the grieving process?

3. Are you practicing adequate self-care through proper rest, nutrition, and stress relief?

4. Have you witnessed any judgment or dismissal over the grief from others? How can you establish genuinely compassionate support?

5. Which areas require more understanding or practical solutions catered to your unique needs?

## Cultural Perspective on Grief

The grieving process often differs significantly across cultures, highlighting the diversity of death rituals, mourning periods, communal coping practices, and beliefs about the afterlife. Exploring cultural contexts provides insight into how your background shapes personal experiences with loss.

In many Latin American and Asian cultures, overt emotional displays like wailing or crying publicly represent deep grief and love for the deceased. Silent, stoic mourning could be seen as insensitive. Comparatively, northern European cultures value muted, composed grieving.

These varied perspectives may explain why I spent weeks openly crying with my family. Yet my close friend from Denmark noticed my public crying as odd as her culture discourages emotional outpourings. Recognizing these differences eased my sense that I may have grieved "the wrong way."

Many African and Indigenous cultures view death as transitioning souls into an ancestral realm where they remain involved in earthly affairs. Mourners find solace in picturing loved ones, observing, or even communicating with them. With my Christian upbringing, imagining an afterlife comforts me when missing Si.

Cultural traditions also encourage community support, illuminating isolation as grief's common, damaging companion. In Judaism, condolence visitors provide meals and company during the mourning period, known as Shiva, to ease loneliness. Asian and Native American cultures host elaborate rituals so entire communities mourn together. Reflecting on my gratitude for kind neighbors who comforted me reinforced that grief links us in universal humanity.

While cultural conditioning doesn't wholly dictate personal grieving, it does offer perspective for finding empathy, meaning, and comfort when facing loss. Understanding these diverse frameworks helps us grasp how upbringing sows seeds of mourning planted in each of our hearts and souls.

Transforming emotional chaos in order helps mourners grasp some control while honoring loss. Through symbolism and ceremony, these rituals harness grief's force for psychological healing.

The therapeutic power of ritual dates back centuries, underpinning religious and cultural mourning traditions worldwide. Lighting memorial candles, wearing ceremonial garb, gathering mementos, or sharing food enables cathartic collective grieving that eases isolation.

Highly personal rituals also carry profound weight. After Si passed, I created a memory box displaying his collar, ashes, and a tuft of his soft fur. Gazing at these mementos helped me to focus the turbulent feelings into bittersweet nostalgia instead of only painful yearning. The intentional practice of reflecting while holding the keepsakes soothed my grieving heart.

Other examples include planting trees or creating memorial gardens with significant plants or objects representing your pet's essence. Compile memory books, photo collages, or tribute videos immortalizes your cherished pet. You may write letters capturing pivotal moments in your bond, seasonally visit meaningful places, share experiences, or observe milestones like birthdays. These are all symbolic gestures.

Rituals aligning with your spiritual belief system can also offer comfort. Some pray while others sense their deceased pets as ever-present guardian angels. Seek inspiration from your own religious or cultural death practices.

Ultimately, any thoughtful, well-orchestrated act that memorializes loss channels grief toward greater self-understanding and solace. Discovering personalized rituals and healing your hidden wounds requires patience, creativity, and deep reflection—but this moving journey toward wholeness proves profoundly rewarding.

# Chapter 6:

# Seeking Support

*Grief is itself a medicine.* –William Cowper

Few journeys demand as much courage as navigating loss's lonely labyrinth of sorrow. By necessity, grief isolates us, yet we all crave companionship to ease our suffering. Seeking empathy and understanding lifts the spirit while building resilience for the road ahead.

In grief's early stages, avoidance and denial often accompany shock, preventing emotional processing and healing. However, patient loved ones will repeatedly extend invitations and communicate an ongoing willingness to connect when emotions are hard. Small gestures like delivering meals, sending cards, helping with practical burdens, or reminiscing about positive memories make darkness feel less ominous.

Support groups offer shared emotions and reminders you aren't alone. Listening to others navigating similar pain normalizes rocky grief responses like outbursts or hopelessness.

While moving forward seems impossible initially, bonding over past joys and funny moments with Si's life eventually roused nostalgic smiles, lifting my gloom. Well-meaning loved ones sat with me in silence when words failed, carrying some light until I produced my own again. Even gentle affection from sympathetic pets soothed my soul.

No perfect formula dictates the "right" grief support—we all need different things. But compassion gives mourners courage. And courage sustains hope faithfully until grief's winter thaws into the warmth of acceptance.

Grieving fully, even messily, ultimately honors the sincerity of love—both giving and receiving. By courageously embracing the swirling storm of emotions battering your heart, you pay righteous homage to an extraordinary soul who blessed your life. There exists no scale measuring the validity of grief based on superficial hierarchical categories—a life altering yours even briefly deserves sincere mourning when lost.

While the acute, crushing pain slowly dulls over time, etched memories ensure your beloved companion lives on through enduring influence on your personal narrative. Gently nurture yourself through the necessary stages of shock, sorrow, and adjustment, knitting broken pieces into an integrated foundation for moving forward. Though nothing replaces your loss, you may discover profound self-revelations and newfound purpose emerging from the ashes of anguish.

Just as the decision to open your heart and home initially to that sweet, innocent creature represented a joyous new chapter, their departure marks a transition into unfamiliar territory. As daunting as charting this foreign landscape appears now, recalling the excitement, nervousness, and wonder of first embracing that new family member sets the stage for rediscovering optimism amidst uncertainty.

# Chapter 7:

# Remembering

*The love of a dog is a pure thing. He gives you a trust which is total. You must not betray it.* –Michel Houellebecq

I still vividly recall the excitement I felt when we first brought him home. This floppy-eared black Lab puppy peered up at me with his big brown eyes, full of curiosity, while his little tail swept back and forth eagerly across our wood floors. As I gently attached the bright red collar around his furry little neck, I swore he smiled at me in that sweet, puppy way. My heart surged with affection for this fluffy little creature, who I just knew would change my life in the best way possible. It took no time at all to realize that although part of our family, I was his person. His loyalty to me shone, and he never hesitated to show it. I spent many hours teaching manners and tricks while, in return, he showed protection and affection. It was a given; wherever I was, Si was within distance.

Over a decade later, the loss of my beloved Si left me reeling in unprecedented grief. Yet reminiscing on the joy of our first days together brings me solace amidst the pain. This chapter invites you to reflect on the origins of the extraordinary bond with your precious pet, from the decision to bring them home to the initial emotional investment and challenges of those early days. By cherishing these nostalgic memories, we continue honoring their enduring pawprint on our hearts.

For many grieving pet owners like myself, the decision to add a pet to one's home and family often stems from a desire for companionship. Perhaps you grew up with childhood pets creating fond memories that left you eager to form similarly heartwarming bonds as an adult. Maybe you observed your own kids pleading for a playmate to snuggle and care for. Or possibly, like many owners, transitioning life stages involving moves, marriages, divorces, or empty nests prompted seeking solace in animal companionship.

Whatever motivated your choice, a pet's delightful presence clearly enriched your life enough to outweigh the work their care required. Your pet likely occupied the roles of not just companion but confidant, therapy partner, or even a child to nurture. Reflecting on those initial visions that compelled you to welcome this precious soul into your home may bring comfort amid loss by underscoring the incredible value they contributed.

## Emotional Investments

Those first few days of adjusting to a new pet's behavior overflow with joyful firsts but require massive emotional investments, too. Patience is tested by sleepless nights catering to needy newborn animals. Frustration mounts as you scrub pet accidents from the carpet and endless hours to train proper behaviors. Yet your commitment never wavers.

With immense pride, you watch your pet blossom over months and years, knowing your dedicated care provided safety, allowing their personality to shine. In turn, they lavish you with unconditional affection in those characteristic ways you adore—sloppy kisses, gentle pounces, soft purring, and loyal gazes conveying pure adoration.

Every snuggle, play session, and shared adventure strengthens attachment bonds that feel unbreakable. No one knows you better than this humble yet magnificent friend, always awaiting your return at day's end. By reminiscing over amusing early memories with your pet, recall the deep emotional roots grounding this extraordinary connection, surviving even death's cruel separation.

While scientifically validating complex human-animal bonds proves challenging, ample evidence affirms pets' positive impacts on human well-being. Numerous studies demonstrate that pet owners exhibit lower blood pressure, cholesterol, triglycerides, loneliness, and depression than non-pet owners. Sharing your home with furry friends also encourages more frequent exercise, outdoor time, and socialization opportunities relative to pet-less peers.

Elderly individuals, singles lacking companionship, and people homebound by illness or disability describe their animal friends as functioning akin to therapy partners, alleviating stress and isolation. Stroking soft fur releases oxytocin hormones, boosting moods similar to hugging loved ones. For children, animal playmates teach empathy and responsibility through nurturing and even emotional self-regulating skills that benefit mental health.

Knowing this substantiated proof of pet benefits lends additional meaning to your grief, underscoring your irreplaceable companion's preciousness. Their enduring gifts involve far more than amusement—they represent peace on days no matter what hardships arise. When darkness descends, conjure memories of your pet's incomparable beauty through steadfast loyalty and wholehearted zeal for life.

# Unexpected Surprises and Challenges

Despite all fantasy-fueled expectations accompanying pet decisions, reality often shocks with unwanted messes, health scares, behavioral issues, and burdensome caretaking requirements. Your initial rosy visions of snuggly, polite, perfectly obedient animals shatter, confronting true pet parenting.

Like actual children, animal companions arrive with unique temperaments and flaws requiring compromise. Cats ignore litter boxes, prompting frantic steam-cleaning sessions. Dogs sideline toddlers with hyper exuberance. That precious eight-week-old kitten you couldn't resist, suddenly morphs into a waking nightmare of shredded curtains and toppled plants after hitting animal puberty.

While their comedy of errors sparks hilarious stories later, in those moments mishaps test patience and even affection for these dependent beings you chose. Yet for all the stress their antics create, your pet's silly personality likely generated much joy and laughter too. If love equals choosing togetherness despite imperfections, then bonding with pets allows some of life's purest love.

Rather than resenting the extra work created, you view it as required nurturing, cultivating an extraordinary friendship incomparable to most human bonds. Just as loving parents withstand sleep deprivation tending newborns, your loyalty and protectiveness safeguarded a vulnerable pet dependent wholly on you. Pride and purpose permeate such moral obligations. However challenging initially, you forged an inimitable connection through perseverance and devotion in those formative early days that withstands time's passage.

# Chapter 8:

# Creating Lasting Memories

The famous American author Joan Didion once wrote, "We forget all too soon the things we thought we could never forget."

When overwhelmed by loss, clinging to memories seems impossible to ask. Yet bravely revisiting even bittersweet moments of joy, humor, and comfort shared with your beloved pet holds tremendous restorative power.

Imagine yourself back on the first night home, cuddling your dozy rescue pup, still wearing that oversized shelter tag. How your fretful kitten calmed only when curled up on your chest listening to your heartbeat, paws kneading contentedly. That first purr. The first trick mastered. First vacation together. First health scare overcome.

Each memory, no matter how small, immortalizes your pet's legacy. Regularly revisiting them recalibrates a grieving brain, fixated on only loss, by reminding you of the blessings that colored every day prior. Use memorable images, videos, and even preserved artifacts like ID tags and worn leashes to gently nudge aside sadness, making space for nostalgic smiles.

When anguish seems relentless, trust in memories' capacity to provide timely solace. Surround yourself with tangible mementos capturing your pet's singular aura to revisit when needing lighthearted moments. In some moments, immerse fully in bittersweet recollections honoring a peerless bond bravely built together. Other times, focus on recalling only the silliest exploits, eliciting the deepest belly laughs.

As days pass, deliberately shift perspective from the finite to the boundless. Let what your beloved pet added to life's beauty, purpose, and wonder eclipse the temporary darkness of their absence. Soon, your pet's enduring gifts emerge each time you conjure their memory to lift your own resilience and compassion. Before long, reflections shine more sweet than bitter in testament to a matchless, abiding friendship conquered.

While first impressions tend to linger, nurturing relationships requires shared investments over time. Yet the origins of extraordinary bonds often contain glimpses foreshadowing that destined depth.

Recall initially gazing into trusting eyes, beaming with new life's innocence. How often were rocky beginnings smoothed by simple acts of affection, like gently stroking soft fur until relaxed sighs signaled blossoming trust? What playful antics elicited the first genuine laughs together?

However, accidentally, your paws and feet collided. Reflect now on moments crystallizing your bond's foundation, illuminating its exceptional strength in even the fiercest storms. Rather than mourning and losing shared tomorrows, celebrate unique yesterdays, making your pet's memory indelible.

# The Role of Nostalgia

The famous Greek physician Hippocrates once called nostalgia "the pain from an old wound."

Memories function akin to double-edged swords reflecting harshness and heartache as easily as warmth or wit. Venturing into the past seeking solace often reopens tender wounds still healing.

Yet remembering beloved pets also revives fading echoes of boisterous barks, soothing purrs, and cold-nose wake-up calls.

Fleeting sensory details, once comprising everyday life, deserve preservation by revisiting hallmark moments together.

While recent loss likely amplifies bitter sorrow, nostalgia develops nuance over time. Today, gazing at images capturing Si's silly puppy antics, like stealing our shoes, makes me first tear up before inevitably chuckling. Similarly, your pet's memory invokes a mosaic of emotions depending on context. Be patient in finding the right balance between avoidance and painful thought until uplifting memories edge out lingering hurt.

Nostalgia activates complex neurological reactions involving perception, emotion, and cognition that remain poorly understood. Research shows that both comfort and pain correlate to reminiscing's impact. Focus on curating collections of cherished moments that elicit more amusement than melancholy. Tap supportive loved ones to contribute their vibrant memories of your pet at their shining best.

Gradually, the kaleidoscopic colors of nostalgia shift from darker to lighter hues. Each fond reflection becomes a stepping stone, crossing the tumultuous waters of early grief toward the peaceful shore where love's permanence dwells. There, your remarkable pet still scampers by your side, making playful mischief, reminding you that laughter heals all wounds given time and courage to remember.

Despite the rollercoaster of raising a new pet, from starry-eyed dreams to messy reality checks, those early days cement the foundations for a life-enriching friendship. Recalling frustration over shredded slippers or steep vet bills, through the lens of love, recolors such memories with affection. For hardships faced together only strengthened extraordinary attachment bonds, distinguishing these relationships as hallowed treasures.

Rather than dwelling on the loss, allow your remarkable pet's first moments of kindling laughter within your life to resurface again. Their beginnings are beautifully intertwined with your own adventures. Navigating pivotal phases with this devoted, unconditionally loving soulmate ever by your side. Though the sting of missing your cherished friend remains, appreciate knowing that by providing them with their very best life, you made wonderful memories that death can never erase.

So now stow the tissues and permit therapeutic laughter to emerge from behind sorrow's mourning veil. As sunlight always peeks through even the most ominous clouds if given time, so too do comedic pet escapades deserve fond remembrance after cruelty's undeserved nightmare. Healing means rediscovering your beloved friend's talent for amusement amidst the grief. It's what your extraordinary pet would want—for laughter to have the last word.

# Chapter 9:

# Sharing Stories

There exists no greater soothing of sadness than discovering mutual understanding through sharing stories—especially involving departed beloveds. Rather than wrestling grief alone, confide treasured memories showcasing your precious pet's personality and impact on your life.

Listeners offering laughter and tears in response affirm that you and your pet touched others, too. This interconnectivity through storytelling combats trauma's isolation, allowing grief to be gradually released. Be thoughtful about selecting empathetic audiences who won't critique your very real and messy mourning process.

While certainly bittersweet initially, engaging in commemorative story-sharing lays the groundwork for relief through cathartic release. Focus first on lighter exploits featuring your clever pals silly antics, playful routines or endearing quirks that never failed eliciting smiles. Before long, a community of support rallies around these remembrances building resilience against devastating loss through shared strength.

When ready, revisit more personal moments illuminating your pet's immeasurable influence as a confidant and nurturer, with intimate understanding during life's pivotal events. Recognizing choosing vulnerability in order to process pain facilitates authentic healing. Finally, weaving tragedies like illness and accidents, narrated into heroic outcomes, emphasizes courage in conquering trauma through unrelenting loyalty and love on both sides.

These shared emotions convert mourning into powerful meaning-making, whereby a remarkable pet's enduring legacy extends beyond one personal sphere, touching unforeseen lives for generations. Though gone too soon physically, your beloved pet's spirit persists, lifting burdens and providing comfort through ever-evolving stories, solidifying their magnificent pawprint on your grateful heart.

## Reflection Questions:

1. What initially motivated you to bring your pet into your life?

2. How did you feel the moment you first saw your new pet? Describe the experience in vivid detail.

3. What surprises or challenges did you encounter adjusting to life with your new pet? How did you overcome them?

4. How can you use happy memories from the beginning of your journey together to find comfort now in your grief?

# Chapter 10:

# I Can Laugh Now

*A good laugh heals a lot of hurts.* –Madeleine L'Engle

Losing my sweet Si and coping with the crushing grief felt like carrying the weight of the world on my shoulders at times. During my darker hours of despair, when I thought joy might never return, a friend reminded me, "Laughter still exists as an option—go find it."

Her words nudged me to open photo albums filled with silly images of Si and all his funny, quirky ways that never failed to make me chuckle. As fond memories replaced painful rumination, I discovered laughter's astonishing capacity to lift the spirit and unite the grieving heart with joy.

This chapter explores restorative blessings amidst sorrow through silly pet stories evoking amusement and research on humor's therapeutic effects. By collecting your own humor-filled pet memories as treasured keepsakes, alongside mine honoring clever Si, may we continue discovering resilience and light even on grief's stormiest seas, confident laughter persists sailing right beside us.

## The Healing Power of Laughter

Legend tells of crestfallen Adam pleading with God after realizing every creature except man possessed built-in defenses like fangs or wings. But God gifted Adam an invisible weapon protecting better than any tooth or talon—a sense of humor spreading contagious laughter, ensuring no hardship faced alone.

Even medical science confirms laughter's astonishing physical and emotional impacts. Studies show joyful laughter reduces stress hormones, stimulates circulation, enhances oxygen intake, and releases pleasure-inducing endorphins acting as natural painkillers. Psychologically, humor reframes perspectives, builds comradery through contagion, strengthens resilience against adversity, and communicates empathy, especially regarding taboo topics.

Simply put, sharing laughter makes living's inevitable pains easier, one breath at a time. In grief's paralysis, laughter offers freedom's first steps toward reclaimed joy.

# Humor as a Coping Mechanism

Coping strategies that people instinctively employ to manage stressful emotions or situations represent attempts to regain emotional equilibrium through adaptive behavioral responses. Humor is classified as an emotion-focused coping mechanism, and it lessens distress by infusing scenarios perceived negatively with perspectives eliciting amusement and feelings of levity.

According to researchers, humor operates therapeutically by first alleviating physiological and psychological symptoms of stress when anxiety-induced overthinking gives way to initial bursts of laughter. Then, as laughter's contagion takes hold among others, it builds social cohesion through shared emotions. By finding delight amidst hardship, humor also strengthens the resilience needed to endure loss.

Studies examining trauma survivors, including bereaved pet owners, indicate healthy styles of humor focusing on lightheartedness versus hostility correlate with a lower incidence of grief complications like depression or complicated mourning. So, while certainly no solution for mourning, sprinkling comedy amidst tragedy helps grieving souls catch their breath when emotional tides threaten to capsize us.

# Laughter Through Tears—a Journal Exercise

When waves of grief leave you feeling saturated in sorrow, try this journaling exercise below to help introduce some moments of lightness through fond, funny memories of your beloved pet.

Gather any artifacts or photos that never fail to make you smile while picturing your pet, especially during silly misadventures. As you review these keepsakes, jot down every detail you can recall about the scenario eliciting belly laughs at the time. What exactly did your pet do that struck you so funny? How did it make you feel witnessing their spirited antics? What made that particular incident so humorous compared to other exploits?

After revisiting several special funny episodes through thorough journal descriptions, close your eyes while holding a cherished photo. Replay your favorite laugh-out-loud scene vividly in your mind's theater. Slowly allow delightful emotions associated with that golden memory to ripple through you until the warmth of nostalgic joy emerges to calm any lingering grief-induced tension or sadness.

When grief's frigid loneliness cools our battered spirits, the radiance of fond memories never fails to warm hearts frozen by sorrow's bitter winds. Each time merriment thaws grief's isolating chill, another epiphany blossoms, insisting love always prevails.

# Chapter 11:

# The Quirks and Eccentricities

Like a fingerprint's swirling ridges, which render every human unique, little behavioral quirks also distinguish animal companions as exceptional souls blessing our lives in one-of-a-kind ways.

What initially struck you as delightfully distinctive about your pet? Was it the silly sideways excitable scamper when you produced their leash for walks? Their habit of flopping down insistently atop your feet while working at home, showing steadfast commitment to keeping you company? The way they sang passionately, if pathetically, along with TV show theme songs?

Such endearing idiosyncrasies capture your pet's essence more indelibly than any portrait by immortalizing little details defining their vibrant, dynamic character, which you only fully appreciate when loss forced recollection. By compiling records purposefully preserving these priceless personality hallmarks, your pet's enduring legacy persists even beyond death.

So, alongside customary condolence cards received, proudly display any artwork, writings, or media commemorating your pet's special quirks for all to enjoy, too. Not only does this demonstrate celebrating your pet's beautiful uniqueness and your shared adventure together, but it also fosters priceless opportunities for much-needed comic relief as others entertain you with funny stories of their own beloved pets. These amusing exchanges forge an invaluable support network, reminding no one grieves alone.

Laughter eternally bonds the bereaved as we trade tales showcasing our irreplaceable companions' delightful diversity. However desperately our hearts may break bidding temporary farewells, the recollections always revive a faith that humor and devotion will carry us through even the most devastating of trials together.

# Funny Pet Stories

To spark laughter amid sadness, let's remember amusing anecdotes showcasing our pets' delightful spirits. I'll start by sharing a classic Si story.

Si loved going on walks; it was the highlight of his day. He'd put the leash in his mouth like he was actually the one taking me on the walk. However, Si also loved squirrels. We were halfway through our relaxing walk when, out of the corner of my eye, I noticed a squirrel darting to an upcoming tree about a block away. Unfortunately for me, Si was already on point and ready to attack. He jerked so fast that down I went. Before I realized we were on chase, he dragged me through the entire block without hesitation. I was so mad and embarrassed by the time he stopped and I was able to contain myself. It took all I had not to scold him at the top of my lungs. He was so proud of himself for getting us so close this time to conquering the squirrel chase that he didn't even notice my rage. As I scurried off to get us out of view of any possible watchful eyes, all I could do was laugh at how that whole event had just actually happened. I was dragged a good city block by my faithful friend, all for the love of a squirrel… What a traitor.

Poor Si never got his squirrel, but he tried to the bitter end.

What funny or heartwarming stories can you think of to light your sadness about your furry friend? Compiling these quirky stories into a communal celebration of our extraordinary animal friends' antics comforts the grieving heart.

Humor's subjective nature means one person's comedic scenario fails, amusing another. But certain pet exploits elicit such belly laughs even strangers relate. Capturing such moments through photos, videos, or written descriptions memorializes humor we can revisit when needed. Use smartphones to document amusing incidents and catalog them into albums, revisiting when you need laughter's healing. Soon, your grieving days overflow with happiness, recalling their silly antics.

Shared laughter builds powerful social bonds, easing struggles faced alone. In grief support groups, humorous stories bring catharsis and optimism. Listening to others navigating sorrow reminds you that you aren't alone while trading tales invoking laughter lifts spirits through contagious endorphins and comradery.

Immortalizing delightful memories through diverse creative mediums infuses sadness with the celebration of special bonds once blessing our lives. Perhaps organize collaborative community art exhibits showcasing works honoring pets' spirited legacy. Not only do such creative expressions foster laughter and connection, but they also continue your remarkable animal friend's gift of happiness, surviving even their physical absence.

Just as reminiscing over Si's puppy photo album transports my tear-streaked face into nostalgic smiles, may humor and art we craft from relics of amusing exploits together lift heavy grief for you as well, my friend. Until we meet our dear furry confidants again, let our shared laughter and creativity kindle that immortal light of love no darkness can extinguish.

They say laughter equals inner sunshine, thawing even the iciest sadness when given a warm reception. Though the ache of missing a cherished friend remains acute, appreciate knowing that you provided their very best life and you made wonderful memories death can never erase.

So, stow the tissues and permit therapeutic laughter to emerge from behind sorrow's mourning veil. For as sunlight always peeks through even the most ominous clouds if given time, so too do comedic pet escapades deserve fond remembrance. Healing means rediscovering your beloved friend's zest for life amidst the grief. It's what your extraordinary pet would want—for laughter to have the last word.

As we continue along this winding path, making sense of loss, explore the extraordinary familial bonds we forge with our devoted animal companions. From first joining our households as awkward newcomers to earning the noble status of sibling, child, or grandparent through years of affection, our pets transform strangers into kin. By remembering the profound role they played within our families, we summon the courage to appreciate their enduring gifts even in their absence.

## Reflection Questions:

1.  What is one of your all-time favorite silly or amusing memories with your pet? Revisit that story vividly in your journal, capturing every detail possible related to the scenario eliciting such hearty laughs through their spirited antics.

2.  Besides funny misadventures, what other little quirks or eccentric qualities set your pet apart as an extraordinary, one-of-a-kind soul? Compile descriptions capturing your pet's singular aura—the way their eyes crinkled when happy or how they snuggled up to comfort you when sad.

3.  Exchange treasured "quirky pet tales" with trusted friends experiencing similar loss of beloved animal companions. After sharing lighthearted stories and a good laugh, discuss what you appreciate about having a judgment-free support network amidst turbulent grieving.

# Chapter 12:

# The Family's Role in a Pet's Life

Human families assume immense responsibility for securing pets' welfare through attentive care-taking. Providing shelter, nutrition, and healthcare establishes foundations of trust upon which extraordinary bonds flourish over pets' lifetimes.

Belly rubs meet tactile needs while encouraging positive associations with touch. Celebrating milestones like birthdays or marking seasonal holidays incorporates animal family members into traditions through canine-friendly activities. Respectfully mediating conflicts with other household pets helps maintain household harmony.

Equally important as meeting physical requirements, conscientious owners prioritize pets' emotional health, too. Soothing anxious pets during fireworks or thunderstorms prevents reinforcing those triggers' scary connotations. Providing regular affection prevents behavioral issues stemming from inadequate care or attention.

Ensuring proper socialization allows pets to comfortably navigate new environments and unfamiliar people or animals.

While major responsibilities accompany pet parenting, joys exceed any struggles tenfold. Sharing lives with such loving, loyal companions forges unparalleled bonds withstanding almost any hardship. Over the years, their dependability during life's highlights and hardships earns them equal footing within family hierarchies as siblings or even children, warranting equal treatment and enduring loyalty.

Patience allows them to slowly earn more household freedom through behavioral maturity. Accidents become rare; anxious nibbles on belongings fade. Your growing pride outweighs the puppy challenges, making it worth weathering for the delightful companionship that's blossoming. Soon, this new family member offers laughter, purpose, and comfort, exceeding any early inconvenience endured.

By embracing rocky beginnings as opportunities for growth, both pets and humans evolve together.

## Pet Ownership as a Lifestyle

*Dogs are not our whole life, but they make our lives whole.* –Roger Caras

Though some impulsively adopt pets without considering the lifestyle changes required, responsible owners accept animal guardianship's far-reaching impacts. Since domesticated animals rely fully on human caregivers to secure their well-being, priorities necessarily shift to accommodating helpless companions.

Initially, daily routines stretch to incorporate walks, playtime, training, and cleaning, all to accommodate these newcomers. Over months, their needs shape schedules, dictating wake-up times and punctuating workdays to ensure mid-day nourishment. As bonds strengthen through consistent togetherness, their presence feels integral, threading through daily moments.

Pet ownership's responsibilities impact activities and housing decisions for hopefully over a decade. Seeking regular veterinary care maintains health, detecting issues early in hopes treatment proves most effective. Providing nutritious diets tailored over their lifespans protects against obesity and associated illnesses like diabetes or arthritis. Establishing emergency plans for storms, fires, or injuries preemptively reduces risk should disasters arise.

For devoted owners, such sacrifices feel small relative to the rewards of the loving company. The word "home" gains new meaning, coming alive thanks to pitter-pattering paws excitedly circling at day's end as if your arrival completes their world. Cuddling close calms worries no words could adequately soothe. Watching them dream by the fireplace as seasonal celebrations play out. Over time, adaptations feel like privileges—small prices to pay for such profound happiness.

## Creating Lasting Traditions

Like the alluring twinkle of fireflies on long summer evenings, simple rituals illuminate each phase of life's complex emotional journeys—especially involving beloved animal family members. Consider favorite traditions you incorporated involving your precious pet over the years.

Did mealtimes feature placing an extra bowl on the floor filled with their signature food? Maybe leisurely evenings always included your subtle signal, beckoning them to hop into your lap for nightly cuddles. Or perhaps the daily family walk featured your pet tugging eagerly on the leash, guiding the pack's playful adventures.

No matter how silly or small such habits may have seemed, these special rituals strengthen attachment bonds familial in nature, even across species.

My childhood friend Alyssa, for example, still makes homemade doggie birthday cakes annually, even after losing her companion Roxy to lymphoma five years ago. Initially, a whimsical celebration of Roxy's first year was welcomed into the family, and the tradition persisted each birthday for over a decade, becoming symbolic of Roxy's role within the family. Though bittersweet baking solo now, Alyssa described her ritual as a therapeutic reminder that Roxy will always remain an integral member despite her physical absence.

Identify similar meaningfully distinctive traditions you integrated involving your beloved pet. Compile these in a journal with vivid details—sights, sounds, smells, and textures recorded comprehensively. When loss leaves you feeling devastatingly alone, revisiting this tangible history warms the soul with sweet, reminiscing laughter replacing only mournful longing. Much like generations gathering around the family, photo albums allow such humble yet powerful commemorations to resurrect nostalgic joy, bridging past and future with hope.

## The Impact on Children

While all family members grieve losing their animal companion's comforting presence, often younger residents feel the loss most profoundly given the pivotal socioemotional roles pets play in nurturing child development. Studies demonstrate that children in households with pets exhibit higher empathy, emotional intelligence, self-esteem, social skills, and responsibility than in home environments where humans exclusively model behavior.

Unlike parents burdened by stress or peers consumed with competition, pets offer patient companionship, celebrating children's authentic selves with unconditional affection. This consistent positive regard teaches self-acceptance and self-worth to children still constructing identity. The absence of this special ally providing sensitive support through pivotal coming-of-age years leaves children doubly disadvantaged both by losing nurturing friendships and stable outlets regulating intense emotions.

While certainly no human substitute exists to replace this profound pet loss, families demonstrate collective love by rallying compassionately around the grieving young soul. Gentle honesty in balancing pet deaths with reassuring messages that eventually help facilitate mourning without overwhelming children's delicate coping capacities.

Most importantly, encourage children to freely ask questions and express their turbulent feelings without fear of judgment. Losing beloved pets often represents children's first encounters with the gravity of mortality and the darkness grief ushers. In safeguarding spaces where children give words of sorrow, discover resilience, speaking truth even through tears.

# Navigating Loss Together

Grappling with grief after losing extraordinary animal family members plunges households into collective mourning each member experiences uniquely. Try not to isolate but to support through turbulent healing.

Younger members may undergo dramatic behavioral shifts in the aftermath of trauma and require delicate guidance in making sense of death's permanence. Stoic spouses hide bottled hurt, sparing extra suffering. Sandwiched elders silence their own profound pet-related grief, comforting anguished grandchildren instead. Navigating this precarious dance demands careful communication, empathy, and patience.

# Reflection Questions:

1. How did welcoming a new pet transform dynamics in your family or household? What adjustments did members make to welcome them?

2. Share a story exemplifying a challenge faced in those early days bonding with your new pet. How did overcoming it strengthen your relationship?

3. In what ways were you able to provide an enriching, nurturing environment and lifestyle for your beloved pet's growth and happiness? How did they reciprocate love back to the family?

4. What are some favorite memories exemplifying your extraordinary companion at their shining best within your family adventures and moments?

# Conclusion:

# The Legacy of a Family Pet

That one dutiful family member occupying the role of playmate and confidant in equal measure undoubtedly merits honor as MVP even once physically gone from your homes and lives. What silly facial expressions or spirited antics still ignite chuckles during reminiscing?

- Can you picture the sparkle animating their eyes when your car pulled into the driveway after a long day?

- Do you remember cuddling in fur sprinkled generously with kisses following tough losses, nearly buckling your spirit on those bittersweet days?

Precious pets become woven into the very pulse, rhythm, and rituals of family dynamics—another strand of DNA somehow scandalously more unconditional in affection than any human counterpart. Losing such sacred heart connections leaves gaping voids where their steadfast loyalty once stood.

Yet genuinely honoring a beloved pet's rightful role within your family's narrative means more than tearful farewells.

However you choose to pay homage, know that your extraordinary pet's enduring legacy outpaces even genetic blueprints—for love measured by devotion leaves the longest-lasting legacy of all.

In closing, remember your pet, hold them in your heart as they did yours, and most importantly, be joyful in the fact you were able to experience such friendship and love.

You were a good boy, Si.